RuLes foR WiVes

RULES FOR WIVES

Sara Beth Andrews and James Dale

**Andrews McMeel
Publishing**

Kansas City

02 03 04 05 BRG 10 9 8 7 6 5 4 3 2

Library of Congress Cataloging-in-Publication Data

Andrews, Sara Beth.
    Rules for wives / Sara Beth Andrews and James Dale.
        p. cm.
    ISBN 0-7407-1885-1
    1. Wives—Psychology. 2. Wives—Attitudes. 3. Husbands—
Psychology. 4. Marriage—Psychological aspects. I. Dale, Jim, 1948– II. Title.
HQ759 .A53 2001
306.872—dc21   2001044579

Book design by Holly Camerlinck

RuLes foR WiVes

Introduction

Here they are, the rules you've been waiting for. The rules you didn't even know existed. The rules no one told you about when you went on a date that led to a date that led to an engagement that led to "I do."

Your mother never sat you down and said, "Sweetheart, in marriage, let the man hold the remote control. It gives him the illusion of power." Your married girlfriends never took you aside and said, "Beer is to guys what flowers are to women." Your old roommate never confided, "Sometimes you have to fake it with your husband—that is, your interest in sports."

Nobody ever said there were rules or guidelines or laws you'd need in order to deal with the opposite sex. You thought this wife-husband stuff came naturally.

Wrong! There's nothing natural about it. Why do you think they call them the "opposite" sex? They're weird. A species unto themselves.

You have to know the rules. For instance:

Admire his power tools and he'll worship the patio he built for you to walk upon.

Buy him a satellite dish and he'll do the dishes for the rest of his life.

Compromise and you'll always get your way. (It only sounds like a contradiction.)

So, thanks to thousands of wives (and their husbands) here are the pretested, proven, immutable laws for dealing with/handling/steering/shaping/molding/loving/and, if need be, hypnotizing the opposite sex.

If you follow these rules, will you have a perfect marriage? Who knows? What is a perfect marriage, anyway? Yours, mine, or someone else's? But the rules can't hurt. Proof? Rule One: "You Win."

You Win

You know you're in charge. He knows you're in charge. Don't flaunt it.

Give Him the Illusion of Power (aka the Remote Control)

For some reason, holding the television remote control will give him the feeling he actually has power. *Click*—He's the one who determines whether you watch *NBC Nightly News* or CNN. *Click*—He's the one who decides if it's Leno or Letterman. *Click*—He's the one who picks between *Survivor* and *Dharma and Greg*.

Big deal. You're the one who picks where you live, where you go on vacation, how you invest your money, and who your friends are.

Let him click until his thumb wears out.

Compromise

(VERB: TO MANIPULATE SO AS TO GET EXACTLY WHAT YOU WANT)

It has been said that woman's role throughout history is to compromise (especially wives with husbands). She gives in. She makes concessions. She settles for less. She sacrifices. She puts her own wishes second to those of others. Some consider this a historic subservience to males. Some think it is the innate selflessness of females.

What it is is great PR. (Thanks to Eve, Cleopatra, Queen Victoria, and Oprah, to name a few of the all-time great "compromisers.")

Women/wives don't really give in or sacrifice or concede. You actually command, determine, influence, rule! Subtly. Smoothly. Coolly. (Unlike men who demand and yell while perspiring.)

But keep up the public relations. "Compromise" sounds a lot better than "absolute, all-powerful, dictatorial control."

3

FAKE IT.
HE WON'T KNOW.

Pretend you're interested in sports. When he *oohs*, you *ooh*. When he *aahs*, you *aah*. When he *boos*, you *boo*. When he stands up and yells, *"YES! YES! YES!"* . . . you stand up and yell, *"YES! YES! YES!"*

You don't have to know that the ref made a bad call or the coach sent in a dumb play or the game just went into sudden death overtime (no one actually dies) or the wild card playoff spot is riding on this play or the MVP isn't wearing his lucky sweat socks or what a "pick" is (not a piece of wood you stick between your teeth) or how many points a safety is (two) or that the pitcher just "dusted off" the batter but he didn't look dusty to begin with or why they pour

cold, sticky Gatorade on the coach who wins but leave the losing coach warm and dry. You don't have to know any of it. You just have to follow his lead.

There is no better way to bond with your husband than to experience simultaneous thrills . . . even if you're faking yours.

Don't Be His Mother

He already has one. She's either perfect or his demon. You don't want to be either.

You may never make a sandwich like she did (tuna fish chopped extra fine with pickles but no celery, lettuce but not the weedy kind, mustard on top, mayonnaise on bottom, crust trimmed, lightly toasted, cut on the diagonal).

But on the other hand, you may never be the reason he chews his fingernails, grinds his teeth, gets migraines, breaks into a sweat at the sight of green beans, hates germs, or goes to a shrink trying to figure out why nothing he's ever done is any good.

Be his wife, his romance, his partner, his friend, his lover. You can share life, children, hopes, fears, frustrations, struggles, changes, and each other.

No Trick "am I Fat?" Questions

No matter how you ask it (and there are a million ways), "Am I fat?" has no good answer. It's a trap, a trick, a lure, an invitation to disaster pretending to be conversation, a marital atomic bomb waiting to detonate, doom in the form of a question.

Play fair. Never ask any version or variation of the following:

Do I Look Like I've Gained Weight?

The basic no-win question. "No" means he's lying and you know he's lying so why would he lie to his own wife? "Yes" means he has a death wish.

Is everyone Here tHinneR tHan I am?

Phony comparative survey version of the basic "weight" question. "Yes" isn't an option (see above). "No" leads to, "Okay, who is and who isn't?" This path is a minefield: One step and he blows up.

Is my DRess too tiGHt?

Oh sure, blame the dress. Nice try. It's just the "weight" question in disguise. "No" means he likes tight, slutty-dressing women, like the woman across the room he wants to run away with. "Yes" means you're fat and he's an insensitive slug.

Is my Butt as BiG as it LooKs in tHe ReflectioN?

Just an attempt to shift the issue to the mirror. Another minefield. There are two butts. The real butt and the reflection butt. But there is no good butt. If he says, "No, your butt is not as big as it looks in the reflection," it means your butt *looks* big, which is just as bad as it *being* big. If he says "Yes," well, he might as well shish kebab his own heart.

CaN YoU See tHe GRaY IN mY HaiR?

It doesn't seem like the "weight" question, but you know it is. In fact, it's worse. You're really asking, "Am I getting fat *and* gray?" If he answers "No," it means he wasn't paying enough attention to you to notice the gray, which is obviously right there above your fat neck and arms. "Yes" means your head is basically a gray hat and you look like his grandmother, probably a fat grandmother.

Do mY WRiNKLes sHoW?

Even he knows enough not to answer this one. Wrinkles are most obvious when they cut across what? Fat.

Do YoU tHiNK tHat WomaN acRoss tHe RooM is seXY?

This is the fat question disguised as the affair question. "No" means he's lying. Of course that woman is sexy. She's wearing half a dress and no bra. "Yes" means he wishes he could run away with her and is actually having an affair with her in his imagination, the unfaithful creep!

WOULD YOU RATHER BE WITH A SMART WOMAN OR A BEAUTIFUL WOMAN?

Ah, the hypothetical, thoughtful, philosophical question. What if? Why? Let's discuss. Red Alert! Unfair! Unfair! Unfair! It's the fat question! Only now it's worse than Sophie's Choice. She only had to decide between her children. "Smart" means you don't look so good—because you're fat—but you might be helpful in the event of a nuclear war. "Beautiful" means he's just a shallow, superficial, testosterone-driven male who thinks you're fat!

You know the trick questions. You know there are no good answers. But you'll probably give in and ask one of them anyway. Why? Because wives have been asking the "Am I fat?" question (and its variations) since prehistoric times.

Hey, Zog, do I look heavy in this ocelot dress?

A little. Why don't you wear the T-rex outfit?

Oh, so you're saying I'm as big as a dinosaur. Fine, go to the invention of the wheel celebration without me.

And then Zog spent the rest of the night hunting for pretty moss to give her to make up. Avoid the questions and you will avoid an age-old marital problem: sleeping in separate caves.

BeeR IS to Men WHat FLoWeRS aRe to Women

either one is a little treat that can make someone's day. A dozen fresh buds or a dozen fresh Buds. There are other similarities. You can put both in a glass container. When first opened, they're great, but soon they droop and go flat. There are many varieties of each: organic, hybrid, and hothouse; domestic, imported, and microbrews. And you don't need a special occasion to get them. Just because it's 176 days until the Super Bowl.

So pick him up a six-pack or two. It's a great way to say "I was thinking of you." He may weep.

Learn Grunt Language. Grunt Back.

Your husband may speak to you in mumbles, snorts, and grunts. This doesn't mean he's ignoring you or treating your conversation casually. This is his way of talking. If he makes a mouth noise, he's paying attention and answering you. It's just in a language you don't understand.

He is speaking Grunt, a dialect of English passed on from father to son. "Uhn" means "I agree, the next-door neighbor is obnoxious." "Ngh" means "No thanks, I don't care for any more pot roast." "Hnnh!" means "Wow, I didn't know that. Glad you told me." Listen to the sounds carefully. Eventually you will distinguish the difference between "mghn" and "whaa." In time you even learn to answer his "hnghn" with your "ynuh."

And you two will achieve what all couples strive for: communication.

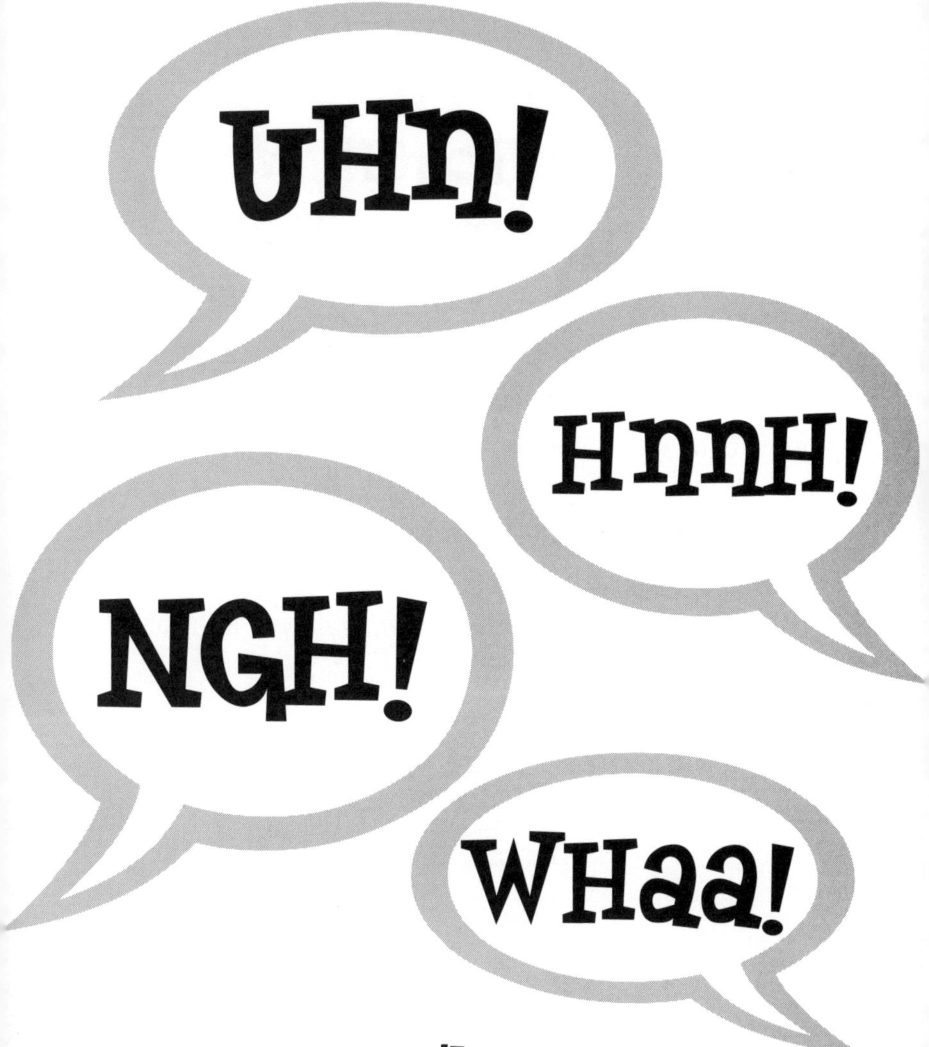
UHn!
HnnH!
NGH!
WHaa!

Get in Touch With Your Inner Male

Deep inside you is a cruder, less sensitive, sweatier self. Find it and you will understand your mate better. You will get why he yells at referees on television who can't hear him. You, too, will give obscene hand gestures to #*!@%**!! drivers. You may even pat your belly fondly as if it's a good friend. You will have gas and you will snore.

Getting in touch with your inner male will bring about two results:

You will truly relate to your mate.

You will appreciate being a higher life form: woman.

Save Dance Coupons

Dancing is a catchall term for anything husbands hate to do. Hated activities (going to fabric stores, picking out wallpaper, getting up early, talking at breakfast) vary from husband to husband, except for dancing.

Almost all husbands hate to dance. And for good reason. At any given moment in history, there are only seven men who can dance well. Right now there are Gregory Hines, Mikhail Baryshnikov, and the five members of 'NSync. All other men just shuffle their feet, have arm spasms, do the lower lip bite, and wait for the song to be over. No wonder they hate it.

So if you like dancing, do you give it up? No, save it up like coupons, only to be used now and then. New Year's. A bar mitzvah. Your class reunion. Same goes for other stuff he hates. Save it up. How often do you really have to pick out wallpaper?

eMPOWeR Him

Buy him power tools. Men love power tools. Why? Because they are tools and they have power. They can drive holes in stuff. Cut stuff. Grind and bore stuff. Make stuff. Fix broken stuff. (More often, break fixed stuff.)

Whenever a husband is using his power tools, he is happy. He is turning a plank of wood into a plank of wood with holes in it. If all male world leaders had power tools, there would be no wars.

Buy Your Caveman a Barbecue Grill

Men like tools. The bigger, the better. (See section on "Empower Him.") And a barbecue grill is the biggest, most powerful tool there is. It has sheet metal, racks, dials, gauges, switches, fuel, and best of all, flames. It's like an airplane cockpit attached to a blast furnace. With it he can turn flesh into food.

He is man. He is macho. He is caveman: *Catch mountain lion. Heave carcass onto fire. Eat.* Okay, so it's more like: *Form ground round into patties. Season with flavor pouch. Sear, flip, sear. Serve with endive salad and a crisp Bordeaux.*

Give him a great barbecue and he will happily stand in driving rain, hail, sleet, or a blizzard cooking dinner on his grill. You will eat well without cooking or cleaning up. (Why do you think cavewomen invented fire in the first place?)

Go to a Car Chase Movie With Him

Why would you waste more than two hours in a theater watching some crazed macho nut (the good guy) drive 175 miles an hour, smashing through construction barricades, garbage cans, flower stands, police barriers, brick walls, pickup trucks, buses, and lots of plate glass windows, hot on the trail of some other deranged nut (the bad guy), who happens to have the stolen nuclear whatever in his car, until the first nut finally crashes into the second nut's car and saves the world by turning off the nuclear whatever with only 5-4-3-2-1 seconds to go on the timer?

Because then your husband will go with you to see the latest remake of *Little Women*. It's life; it's the testosterone-estrogen trade-off.

Remember your old Boyfriend?

Okay, now forget him. Your husband doesn't want to know about him, see him, meet him, hear about him, or even be aware he exists. Sure, your husband might smile and pretend to be interested, but he actually hates your old boyfriend.

You don't believe it? Okay. Think of it this way: Your husband has an old girlfriend. Do you want to meet her, hang out together, laugh at her little jokes, see how gorgeous she is, how successful she's become . . . Had enough?

a WORD aBOut
FLiRtiNG: DOn't

Sometimes it's tempting. It might make you feel young and sexy for a moment or two.

But is it worth it? Your husband will notice. And he will feel bad. And jealous. And hurt. And then you will feel bad. Really bad. And guilty. And you'll think you deserve some awful punishment like in those old movies where the convict gets caught trying to escape from prison and gets put into the solitary, dirty, rat-infested "hole" for a month just because you flirted with some guy you don't even care about.

So, if you get the urge to flirt, rent an old prison movie instead.

Remember Key Dates

 **T**he NBA draft

 **M**arch Madness (easy to remember)

 **T**he Super Bowl

 **O**pening day of baseball season

 **J**oe Montana's birthday

Listen to His Work Stories

They will be boring. You will know the endings before he tells them. Eighty-six percent fall into the My-Boss-Is-a-Jerk category. The other 14 percent are equally divided into something to do with inventory, the busy season, computer glitches, and shipments/invoices/tracking numbers.

Be understanding. He is probably underappreciated. Overappreciate him.

Get Him a Satellite Dish

Satellite dishes are huge. They're ugly. They look like some lunatic (who lives at your house) is trying to make contact with aliens. But they get seven hundred channels, twenty-four hours a day, seven days a week, from every country on Earth and several other planets: Every movie ever made (don't miss the winners of the Lithuanian Film Festival). Breaking news from all seven regular continents, plus Atlantis. Games, scores, highlights, and locker room interviews on every sport from Major League Baseball to Asia Minor League Snake-Hurling, from the Big Ten to the Antarctica Two, from the Super Bowl to Vatican Touch Football (always bet on the pope's team), from the Stanley Cup to Boris's Potato Race. Plus the hit sitcoms of Greece (*Don't Touch My Souvlaki*), soap operas of Tibet (*All My*

Sherpas), game shows from Syria (*Who Wants to be an Oil Sheik?*), Scandinavian reality shows (*How Cold Can You Stand It?*), and shopping channels from the OPEC nations ("Call now and get a sterling silver oil dipstick"). Basically you get every show there is, from everywhere, all the time.

Get your husband a satellite dish. It's like giving him cable television on steroids. Hand him the remote. He is the God of TV. He is truly, deeply, spiritually fulfilled.

Now, you may ask why your husband wants or needs this much television. Why do you need so many shoes?

Don't Let Him Count your Shoes

Speaking of shoes, the number of pairs you have will never make sense to him. Basic husband logic says no one needs more than two, maybe three, pairs of shoes. (Black, brown, and sneakers.)

He will not be able to comprehend so many kinds of sandals. Why thongs, roped, flip-flop, ergonomic, and painful? Or high heels of every height by 1/8 inch increments. Or pointy toes, square toes, round toes, and no toes. Same goes for straps. And all those colors. He will not see the necessity for peach shoes. And turquoise is doubtful. He won't appreciate the subtlety of the white spectrum: bright white, off-white, milky white, starch white, eggshell, ecru, sand, salt, powdered sugar white, etc. And he'll be baffled by the concept of different blacks. "Isn't black black?"

Don't try to explain the shoe deal. His mind can't process it. Shoes aren't a rational, reasonable, sensible thing. They're a need.

He won't get it. Just ask him, "Honey, why do you need all those television channels?"

eXPLain SHoPPinG
(It's LiKe aiR-
ConDitioneD GoLf
WitH CReDit CaRDs)

Men do not innately understand the concept of wandering around retail establishments, picking up items, touching fabric, pondering colors, holding clothing in front of a mirror, taking multiple items into a dressing room but not trying them all on, trying a size that isn't your size, seeing what's new, checking sale racks, comparing price tags, monitoring markdowns, final markdowns, and clearance prices, the difference between "just browsing" and "thinking about it," calling another store to see if they have a different

color/size/style/cut/weight/weave, asking the salesperson who is a complete stranger how something looks, buying and returning, getting a store credit, and going back and buying the thing you returned after checking every other store and finding out it was really what you wanted in the first place.

So explain it to your husband. If you have his full attention and he has an open mind and you are patient and careful in your explanation, he still won't get it.

Instead just tell him it's golf. Golf is every bit as illogical, addictive, and evidently, therapeutic: Prop a small sphere on a wooden pedestal; whack the sphere with a long stick; walk (or ride in a little car) down a green path through woods, around trees and fake lakes in search of the sphere; find it buried under a rock next to a thorny bush; continually smack it in the general direction of a flag sticking out of a hole in the ground up on a perfectly manicured miniature

lawn; once there, tap the sphere toward the hole until it falls
in; count (and sometimes lie about) how many
hits/shots/strokes/nudges/whiffs it took to get the sphere
into the hole; do it eighteen times; and afterward rehash
every single hit or miss and what mighta, coulda, shoulda
happened on each hole "if only . . ."

Then, take your husband along on your next shopping
trip. And go play golf with him. One of two things will happen: 1) He still won't get shopping and you won't get golf
but you'll both get that your shopping is his golf and his golf
is your shopping and you'll achieve what few couples
achieve: understanding. Or 2) he'll become a shopper and
you'll become a golfer. You two will have no time for anything else, bore many of your friends with your stories of
end-of-season sales and coulda-had-a-birdie-if-onlys, but
you'll be very happy with each other.

Leave Leftovers in the Refrigerator

To husbands, leftovers taste better than original meals. Leftovers are cold. Cold food is very manly. It can be gnawed. It can be eaten with his fingers in front of the TV or leaning over the newspaper or at 3 A.M. when he can't sleep. It can be shoved in his pocket on his way to run errands. And leftovers don't count on his diet. (Foods actually lose calories if not eaten when first served.)

But wait! Isn't this a sexist thing? Assuming that you, the wife, should make all the meals and then leave the leftovers for him, the husband? Yes and no. Yes, you cooking all the meals would be sexist. But no, you don't have to actually cook them. Just buy some food—anything—wrap it in foil and stick in the refrigerator. Presto! Instant leftovers. How thoughtful of you.

GO CAR SHOPPING WITH HIM

He'll be excited. You'll be bored. There is nothing interesting about this activity. All cars are alike. He thinks they're different.

Go with him. Ask a question about gas mileage. Say the vinyl feels like leather. Lift the hood and say "hmmm." Pretend you can tell the difference between ABS brakes and BS brakes.

Just go with him. After all, it only happens about once every four years. (But it really shouldn't be called shopping. It's not fun.)

SHOW Him WHat an IRon IS

That heavy metal thing that makes clothing smooth. Pretty amazing. First the iron, then the vacuum cleaner. A machine that sucks grime into a bag. Wow! Or the dishwasher. Dirty dishes + soap + hot water = clean dishes. A miracle!

It's not his fault if he seems unfamiliar with these things. It's an accident of time. He was raised in the last female-does-the-housework generation. Your job is to welcome him to modern times.

Neatness IS OVeRRateD

So he's a slob. Think of his good qualities: He's a smart slob. He's a kind slob. He's a good-looking slob. He's a thoughtful slob. He's a good father slob. He's a faithful husband slob. He's your slob.

employ Defensive Snoring

He snores. You wake up. You nudge him. He rolls over and stops snoring . . . for a split-second. You put a pillow over your head. Through the feathers and down and foam you hear . . . snoring. You put a pillow over his head. The pillow rises and falls with each snore. You turn on the radio. You hear music . . . mixed with snoring. You punch him. He snores. You kick him. He snores. You cover his nose and mouth, cutting off his oxygen. He stops snoring . . . and breathing. You let him breathe . . . and he snores!

He doesn't wake up from his snoring because it's a proven scientific fact that you don't hear your own snoring. So the only way to sleep through his snoring is by out-snoring him. Your snoring will drown out his snoring. Of course, he may hear your snoring, which will cause him to involuntarily snore louder. Which may cause you to snore louder. And, speaking of science, that's how earthquakes happen.

The important point from a marital-relations perspective is he doesn't *mean* to snore. He's a male. Husbands snore more than wives. Don't hate him for it. Be kind. Be understanding. Be forgiving. Then snore back.

eXPLaiN tHe FeMaLe THeRMoStat THiNG

Most women are colder than most men, most of the time. Women like to set the thermostat between 82 and 106 degrees and sleep under a down comforter.

Then one day, women reach menopause and are suddenly 40 to 90 degrees hotter than men. Women want central air conditioning, window units, overhead fans, and blocks of ice in each room, and they set the temperature in single digits.

But husbands don't know or understand the female thermostat. So they turn the home thermostat down or up, depending on whether it feels too hot or too cool to them. Sensible, right?

Wrong. This makes women/wives go berserk. Crazed. Insane. Wild. Or worse. Depending on the direction the temperature lever is moved, you will become a Full-Body

Popsicle or experience a Human Equator Fit, either one of which causes you to lose legal responsibility for your words or actions.

In fairness to your husband, carefully explain that the female's internal thermostat is 11.5 times more sensitive than the male's. (Okay, the number is made up, but who's going to prove otherwise, some man-scientist?)

What can your husband do? Live with it. Tell him he'll be perspiring for the first twenty years of marriage. Then, during the big change, buy him a sweater or Nordic parka.

But no matter how hot or cold he is, he must not touch that little lever on the home thermostat. He may ask, "Is this fair?" Your reply is, "No, who said marriage was fair?"

Note: If he's desperate, tell him to stick his head in the freezer or rub his hands over the oven.

Set One of Your Car Radio Buttons to the Baseball Station

This small gesture says you're thinking of him even when he's not there. He has his own button on your radio. Third from the left. The baseball station. When he gets in the car, he pushes that button and he hears two things.

First, he hears almost nothing happening in the world's slowest moving sport: "Two down, bottom of the fourth, no score, no one on base, left-handed batter up, pitcher shakes off the sign, catcher gives him another sign, pitcher shakes it off, now he looks in, ready to throw, batter steps out of the box to recheck the first-base coach's signal, here comes the manager out to the mound to call in the reliever or maybe

he just wants to talk with the pitcher, uh-oh, is it starting to sprinkle, which could cause a delay of game . . ."

But he also hears your voice saying that he matters to you. You could climb the highest mountain, swim the ocean, or write a love sonnet and never equal the love communicated by setting the third button from the left to the baseball station.

And the best part is when he's not in the car, you never have to listen to it, unless your day is on overload and you're in the mood for listening to almost nothing happening.

Be youR OWN PeRSON

He'll like you better. You'll like you better. The era of the little woman is over. Actually, it never was.

Don't Be
One of The Boys

He has boyfriends to hang out with, swear with, bet with, spit with, and generally be a boy with. But they can't be what you can be: his girlfriend.

Go to the Ballet with a Girlfriend

Sometimes it's the things you *don't* do with your husband that bring you closer. Like if you don't ask him to go to see people in tights leaping across a stage, maybe he won't ask you to come along to get the car lubed.

You're creating a bond that can last a lifetime.

Be PREPARED to SACRifice a FRieND to tHE GOD of MARRiAGE

You want your friends to be his friends and his friends to be your friends and everybody to be everybody's friend. And, generally, it will work.

But there's going to be someone you care about who just rubs your husband the wrong way. It might be the girl who used to sleep over at your house when you were kids but now has no visible means of support and wants to sleep over at your house again. Or your college roommate who hates men and keeps challenging your husband to arm-wrestling contests. Or the Homecoming Queen from high school who now weighs close to three hundred pounds, the last seventy-five of which came from your refrigerator. Or maybe the snob who married the rich guy with the fancy car, gold watch, and expensive hair who asks what tax bracket you're in. Or that woman from your office who drops over, cries for an hour, and leaves.

There will be someone your husband just doesn't love the way you do. He'll try. But eventually your old friend will be his new enemy. She'll get on his nerves. Or under his skin. Or within a mile of your home once too often. And your husband will have the overwhelming urge for you two to move in the dead of night, without leaving a forwarding address.

That's when you have to reevaluate. Your friend or your husband? Chances are, your old friend is not quite as much fun at a sleepover at age thirty as she was at age eight. Perhaps the Homecoming Queen will have to fuel up somewhere else. And that woman from the office should just stop her damn weeping. Maybe she isn't your best friend. Maybe she isn't even in the top ten. Maybe you shouldn't ask her over to the house, or see her as often . . . or ever. Maybe she is a psychopath.

Besides, there will be a friend of your husband's who you'll want to trade-off for one of yours. *We won't see my friend, the man-hating arm-wrestler, if we don't have to see your old pal, the burned-out hitchhiker.*

Sometimes you just have to throw a friend on the burning altar of marriage.

WHiSPeR NaMeS of PeoPLe He'S SUPPoSeD to ReMeMBeR

Scientists have found that husbands are worse than wives at remembering names . . . and dates, times, addresses, phone numbers, codes, IDs, PINs, and other specific data needed for survival. (It was a female scientist who discovered this and remembered to write it down.)

Evidently, when a man meets another man, he looks at the other man's eyes to see if this new man can be trusted (some old macho thing), blocking out critical information such as his name in favor of this primitive character judgment. The problem that occurs is that even when a man has met a guy who passes the eyes test, he still has no idea what the new, trustworthy man's name is. It isn't until they've met multiple times, and the eye test has been passed several times, that a name registers. (Twin brothers have been known to forget each other's names.)

Worse, when a man meets a woman, his mind simply goes blank. The only woman he would remember is his mother, but he doesn't have to remember her name since she's "Mom."

So when a person approaches who you know and your husband should know, whisper in his ear: "It's Ed. Your boss. The one who pays you." Or "It's your cousin, Charlotte. On your mom's side."

Your husband will be very appreciative. He may even thank you by name.

Do the Details

Make lists, pay the bills, call the plumber. These are the details of life. Husbands are notoriously bad at them. So you can either do the things he doesn't do well (and have him do the ones you don't do well) or you can try to reform all males. But, in the end, some of the bills won't get paid, you'll get finance charges, ruin your perfectly good credit, and never qualify for national political office. It's up to you.

Let Him Have tHe aisLe seat

It's like saying "You are a big, massive, powerful masculine hunk of man." If you're on an airplane, it means that in the case of a disaster, he'll leap from his seat to help others. And if you're at the movies and he got the Giganto-Cola and Tub o' Popcorn Combo, it'll be easier for him to get out to go to the men's room.

Get youR caR WasHeD

This makes husbands very happy. They may be terminally slovenly in every other aspect of their lives but, for some reason (undoubtedly related to engines and testosterone), they like cars and they love clean cars. Make your car shiny and it will show him you care about the important things in life: cars.

If you could either arrange for your husband to have a personal meeting with world leaders from every major country on earth or get your car washed, get your car washed. He will smile from ear to ear. If he were going to meet world leaders, he'd have to get dressed up and wear a tie, which he'd hate.

eat Less THan He Does

He eats until he's full (whatever that means). You eat until you've used up all of your daily "points" on the Hollywood Waste-Away Diet. Not fair? No. But practical.

He's probably bigger. He eats more. You're probably smaller. You eat less. You don't really want to look like him, do you? He doesn't want you to, either. (In case you think this is sexist, do you want him to look like you? Shaved legs, makeup, panty hose, and shoes to match all his outfits?) So, it works for everyone. You're just hungry for the next thirty to fifty years.

P.S. This is not an argument for anorexia, bulimia, lipo-suction, or donating extra chins to the chinless. Everything in moderation, even moderation.

Don't Lift Objects Heavier Than He can Lift

Men, no matter how intelligent, educated, well-rounded, worldly, and enlightened, cannot escape their essential maleness. They measure all success in terms of strength. How much could Einstein bench press? Did Plato have a good left hook? How many push-ups could Shakespeare do?

So if you happen to be a little bit stronger than your husband, keep it to yourself. Ask him to open that stuck jar lid. (Loosen it first.) Insist he carry the suitcases. And don't rearrange the living room furniture when he's out.

Let him think you are awed by his brute power. Even if you really just admire him for his wit, insight, and intellect.

Remember the True Meaning of the Wedding Ring

To you, a wedding ring is a beautiful piece of golden ornamentation symbolic of your eternal bond to each other. To him, it's jewelry, which men don't wear (except men who sell drugs or know how to dance). Or worse, it's a miniature manacle that stands for subservience, enslavement, and the end of all fun. Hence his possible reluctance to wear a wedding ring.

But his reluctance doesn't mean he doesn't love you. It just means he has a deep-seated, psychologically scarring male insecurity neurosis. Like most men. Feel better?

If you really want him to wear a wedding ring, follow this suggestion: Plain. Get him a very plain one. One that could be mistaken for a small car part.

Make Him Wear a Seat Belt and Get a Physical

Men resist things like this. Maybe they think it's not manly. You love him. You want him around as long as possible. Try to get him to do both.

Quit Smoking

Stop today. Right now. Live longer together.

If your husband smokes, this is the one of three things (see seat belts and physicals) you're allowed to pester him to do for you and himself.

BUY HIM ONE GOOD SUIT

every husband should own a good suit. Almost no husbands want to own a good suit. They hate suits. They don't even like sport jackets much. *"Sport jacket? That's a lie. What's the sport part? You can't play a sport in this!"*

But he will need a good suit. So pick it out for him. He doesn't want to shop for it anyway and you don't want him to shop for it. If he did, he'd take the first one he saw. *"Hey, cool, a purple suit, just like the Minnesota Vikings."*

But if you pick it, you'll feel better. And he'll look better. For weddings, funerals, job interviews . . . the really serious stuff . . . the stuff he hates mainly because he has to wear a

suit. But tell him the good part is if he has good suit, he only needs one. For variety, you can just buy him a few neckties.

Of course, he really hates neckties. *"What exactly is the point of a necktie?"*

admire Motorcycles

all men secretly wish they could be Hell's Angels, if only they were allowed to shower regularly and if the Hell's Angel women had more teeth. All men look longingly at motorcycles when they go by. They make little *oooh* or *ahhh* noises that mean "I wish I was on that hog, no responsibilities, wind in my face, going ninety mph to who knows where." All men *think* they want a motorcycle.

So next time a motorcycle goes by, make one of those little noises: *oooh* or *ahhh*. Your husband will turn to you in shock, wondering if you want to be on a big hog, wind in your face, no responsibilities, going ninety mph to who knows where, not showering regularly and without all of your teeth. The thought will be horrifying. And he'll get over thinking he wants a motorcycle.

ask your Husband Out on a Date

Think of a place he'd love to go. Tell him you have something special planned. Buy him a new shirt. Wear something really great. Smell great. Tell him he looks handsome. Don't tell him where you're going. Ask for a quiet table. Order wine. Share your entrees. Have dessert. Pay the bill. Tell him how much you love him.

He'll think you're the coolest human being on earth!

Like the Presents He Gives You

This one is important. Men—especially husbands—feel much more insecure about picking presents for women than women do picking presents for men. It's not a cultural thing or a sexual thing or a role-model thing; it's a genetic thing having to do with Xs and Ys, DNA, RNA, the double helix, and other factors too complex to explain here.

But, continuing along the scientific path, like Pavlov's dogs, husbands are susceptible to behavioral training. If they're told over and over that their presents are not good, they will not try to buy better presents; they will stop buying presents altogether. What is good about this? Nothing.

On the other hand, if they are encouraged, they will eventually buy more and better presents. *"Oh honey, I love this sweater! It's perfect. Well, almost perfect. I'm just going to switch the color from electric magenta to black. And maybe trade the fuzzy wool for the virgin cashmere. And perhaps change the size 18 for a size 6, my size. How did you know I'd love it?!"* What is good about this? More presents.

Husbands want their gifts to be appreciated, not rejected. They are giving you their love. Wrapped up. Open it carefully. Treat it lovingly. Then return it for what you really want because men don't remember what they bought you anyway. It's the thought that counts.

Don't Get Out-Gifted

No matter what you are celebrating—Christmas, Hanukkah, Kwanza, birthdays, anniversaries, Valentine's Day, Sweetest Day, Labor Day (always hard to find the right present)—celebrate with equality. Do not over-gift or under-gift. It will make one of you, or maybe both of you, feel bad.

To be honest, you don't want to *give* an imported cashmere sweater . . . and *get* an apron. (Actually, there should be a national retail law that prohibits aprons from being purchased as gifts.) On the other hand, you don't want to *give* a key chain and *get* a diamond necklace. (Though this is not as bad as getting the apron.)

When it comes to gift giving, set ground rules. You should both agree to spend X dollars this year. Then stick to it. And only exceed your limit a little.

TeLL Him HoW smaRt He IS

Who could ever hear this too much?

TeLL HiM He'S GooD-LooKiNG

Who could ever
hear this too much?

TeLL Him you LoVe Him

The average husband likes to act like he hates mushy stuff. He won't watch sappy TV shows about someone finding her lost mom. He hates birthday cards that are really just long poems. He doesn't know flower names. And he groans at movies where the gross guy suddenly gets sensitive.

He's not very good at expressing his feelings. If you ask him if he loves you, he'll nod his head. But he won't tell you. Someone might hear him. But he likes to know you love him. Tell him. It makes him feel good, secretly. Of course, he won't ever admit it because that would be mushy.

I Love you

71

HOLD HANDS

It feels good. You like it. He likes it. Do it.

Go for a walk

Just be together without anybody else.

TALK to eacH OTHER

as long as you talk, everything is okay.

Don't TRy to CHaNGe Him

He's a person, not a thing. Don't try to make him a little more this or a little less that. Appreciate him for what he is. Human. In love with you. Emotional. Unpredictable. Real.

He's perfect in his imperfection. Like you.

Remember WHy you FeLL in LoVe

every once in a while, when you get aggravated, annoyed, irritated, upset, tired, bored, or testy with each other, stop. Step back. Close your eyes.

Remember the man you fell in love with. How you couldn't resist. You had no control. He was it. You were hooked.

That same man is in the other room. You married him. He's waiting for you.

SPenD Time WitHOut OtHeR COUPLeS

Somewhere along the way, social obligations take over your life. You owe this couple or that one. You haven't seen the so-and-sos in so long. You really ought to go out with the you-know-whos because you haven't seen them since who-knows-when.

You get so caught up in going out with other couples, you forget who you like best. Each other.

It's time to go out without anyone else. Just you two. Wow! Isn't your husband cool? And he finds you so fascinating!

BRAG ABOUT YOUR HUSBAND

Why not? He's probably the best person you know. Tell the world.

TRUST EACH OTHER

Sometimes it's hard. The more you do it, the better it is. Besides, you two are in this life together. Who else are you going to trust?

TeLL tHe TRUtH

You will be tempted to hedge, fudge, waffle, wiggle, or just plain lie about things throughout your relationship. But the truth will always come out. Always. Maybe not today, but tomorrow. Or next week. Or ten years from now. It will come out. For sure. No doubt. Absolutely. You'll forget your own story. A friend will let the truth slip. It'll be on CNN.

Just tell the truth in the first place. About everything. Even if you are just plain wrong. Admit it. Truthfully. Be honest. About everything. No exceptions. The truth. Always. (Unless he asks if it looks like he's losing his hair.)

SeX, Money, anD HouseCLeaninG aRe tHe THRee Major Causes of MaRitaL FriCtion

everyone knows money is an issue. No couple seems to have enough. So you argue. You spent too much. He didn't spend enough. You didn't earn enough. He didn't earn enough. You and he didn't save enough. Enough is never enough. (Unless you have too much, which the rich claim is also a problem, but you doubt it.)

And sex can be an issue. When. Where. How. And, of course, enough is never enough.

But the often overlooked fight causer is housecleaning. You think he's a pig. He thinks (but doesn't say out loud), that you're compulsive. He wants to be able to sit on the sofa even after you've just fluffed the cushions.

You suggest you each make a list of the housecleaning jobs and then divide the combined list equally. He agrees. You make your list. He doesn't make his. You take your list, divide the house in half, give him all the jobs on his side of the house, and take all those on your side of the house. He agrees. You do your half of the jobs. He doesn't do his. He says he doesn't mind if his half of the house is a mess. You do mind. You then clean his half and say he owes you a cleaning of your half next week. He agrees. But he doesn't do it. You clean the entire house and dump everything on his side of the bed. He burrows under it and goes to sleep. Eventually mold, mildew, and fungus begin to build up, mice and other field rodents are attracted, buzzards circle your home, and the city condemns your property. For some reason this leads to a fight.

But there is a solution to all three major marital issues—sex, money, and housecleaning. Save up your money. Do not spend it on nonessentials like food or clothing or heat. Instead, hire a maid to come in once a week and clean both halves of the house.

Now, what will you two do with your spare time? Sex.

Get in Sync

Marriages get out of sync. You want to do something but he doesn't. He wants to do something but you don't. The "something" doesn't matter—eating, shopping, reading, cleaning, calling, sitting, standing, mountain climbing—whatever. You're in the mood for X but he's in the mood for Y. Why? Who knows? The two of you are just off-balance. Out of whack, off kilter, or out of sorts.

How do you get back in whack, on kilter, or in sorts? Skip a beat. You want to do something but he doesn't. Then don't. He wants to do something but you don't. Then do. Just change the rhythm. What you wanted to do or he wanted to do isn't important. Doing whatever you do together is. (Remember, she who marches to the beat of a different drummer marches all by herself.)

FiGHts HaPPen

You're going to fight. Now matter how well matched, easygoing, or compatible the two of you are, it's inevitable. Soul mates, two halves of the same apple, Jimmy and Rosalyn Carter, George and Martha Washington, Yin and Yang, Ben and Jerry—it happens to every twosome. Even the perfect couple, if there is such a thing, has fights (e.g. "Oh, so you think you're perfect, do you?").

Every husband and wife fight about something some time. You want to get dressed up and go someplace nice; he wants to stay home in his underwear. He likes extralong shag carpeting; you prefer bleached hardwood. You want to get up early and go antiquing; he wants to sleep until he becomes an antique. He says let's rent *Rocky XIII*; You say let's rent *Little Women, the Spinster Years*. He wants the

Everything Pizza with extra grease; you want arugula and radicchio salad with no dressing. You say he doesn't like your friends; he says you're right. He wants to watch ESPN Classic Kickboxing Bouts of the '70s; you want to read a romance novel with a picture of Fabio on the cover. You say he doesn't listen to you; he says, "What'd you say?"

You get upset. He gets upset back. Words, louder words, insults, accusations, worse insults, scowls, sulking . . . then long, long, long silences. But there's a good reason.

Fights happen between people who care about each other. People who don't care about each other don't even bother to fight. If your sister-in-law-the-dental-hygienist disapproves of your child-rearing methods, big deal. What makes her an authority, that pretend doctor smock with her name embroidered on the pocket? If the drive-through teller asks who you're voting for and then laughs hysterically, so what? If the package-delivery guy thinks your purse doesn't

match your outfit, who cares? He wears goofy shorts to work.

But if your husband criticizes your mothering, scoffs at your political views, or thinks your purse is ugly, it hurts. Because you don't kiss your sister-in-law-the-dental-hygienist good-night, hold hands with the drive-through teller, or give an anniversary card to the package-delivery guy. You never asked any of those people to spend their life with you or raise your children. You care about your husband and what he thinks. It hurts. It matters. It's supposed to.

Fights are not the end of the world. They don't mean you don't love each other. They mean you do.

Lose

When you do fight, lose. Even if you know you're right. One hundred percent positive. With evidence, eyewitnesses, video cameras, and sworn testimony.

He left the front door unlocked. You locked the front door. You always lock the front door.

He has been known, in the past, to forget to lock the front door (and other doors).

Whoever went out last (your husband) must have left it unlocked.

He's the one who put your home and family in danger.

He says he remembers locking it. But he was definitely the last one out, so . . .

Shut up! The door was left unlocked. So what? Lock it. Go to sleep. Who cares?

And what if you did win the fight? What's the prize? Having your husband annoyed that you proved a stupid point? Is there a trophy commemorating that you proved a stupid point? Can you earn the Olympic gold medal for marital arguing? Are they going to interrupt the evening news with the breaking story of you winning the fight? Will there be a special segment of *Oprah* called "You Being Right"? And if they do any or all of the above, what makes you so sure they won't do all those things for him when he's right?

There's no award for winning fights in marriages. In fact, winning is worse than losing. Lose. Go on with life.

NeVeR aRGUe aBOUt POLitiCS

What difference does it make? (Do you think politicians argue about you?)

Don't Stay Mad

What were you so mad about anyway?

Make Up

This is the only good part about fighting. One of you apologizes (him). Then you kiss and make up. And whatever else.

(If you want to speed things up, accept his apology even before he offers it. As a male, he is programmed to apologize and will assume he did it and be relieved you accepted it so quickly.)

Kiss Good-Night

Make it the one thing you do without exception. Every night. Even if one of you has a fever. Blow each other a kiss. Even if you're out of town. Kiss over the phone. Even if you're mad, kiss. You'll be less mad.

There is nothing bad that ever came from kissing each other good-night. And, frequently, good things come out of it. Like children.

HaVe CHiLDReN

They're the best thing about getting married. Little people that only you and your husband can make.

Take Pictures

They say everything in memory happens to music. The past is better as a reminiscence than the way it really was. Well, maybe. Or maybe it was really good but you can't appreciate it until you look back.

You and your husband are in this life together. It's your book, your movie, your story. Hold on to it. Take pictures. Save mementos. Keep a scrapbook of life. From time to time, relive your journey. Where you've been. What you've been through. Your first house. The old car that sometimes ran. The kids. The pets. The goofy suit and/or bad haircut.

This is your life. Enjoy it, appreciate it, laugh, cry, remember. When things get tough, and they will, you can look back at everything you've been through and know you can make it through anything.

LauGH at NonTRaGiC DisasteRS

Like bounced checks, broken dishes, spilled taco sauce, your husband falling asleep during a musical, falling asleep during an opera, falling asleep while your mother is talking, getting lost and refusing to ask directions, throwing his red socks into the wash with your white underwear, forgetting where you're going this Saturday night.

Laugh because if these things happened to other people, they would be funny. Laugh now because later, when you look back on these things, you'll laugh. Laugh because these things don't matter.

Keep things in perspective. Unfortunately, you will have plenty of things worth getting upset over.

save Money

You will need it sometime. Save it now because you don't know when sometime will be.

evolve

Husbands and wives grow during a marriage. Not always in the same ways. Or at the same pace. Careers, promotions, dumb bosses, firings, moves, births, deaths, bills, savings, wrinkles, spare tires, career changes, car accidents, bad phone calls, vacations, operations, graduations, more moves, new ideas, old friends, gray hair, ear hair, no hair, playing the lottery, paying taxes, losing weight, reading a book, having a dream, facing reality, doing something rash/stupid/bold.

Your changes won't be his changes. His won't be yours. That's okay. Just don't stand still. Don't get stuck in the past. Keep changing. Keep up with each other. Keep evolving. Remember what happened to the dinosaur.

GROW OLD WITH HIM

They say you're only as old as you feel. Well, one day soon, you're going to feel lousy—joints aching, fuzzy eyesight, hard of hearing, and shorter than you were the year before.

Who wants to go through that alone?!

Be an "Us," Not a "Me"

Bottom line: The two of you can either be a) you, the wife. And b) him, the husband. Or you can be the two of you. The partnership. The duet. The united front. The team. The force. Be his other half. Let him be yours.

Why be alone? Go us!

Marriage is
Hard Work. Try.

Like many things in life, marriage is work. You're living with someone else. Sharing space, soap, and feelings. You have to understand things you don't really understand (some things have to do with that X and Y chromosome thing.) You have to listen, even when you're all listened out. You have to be patient when your fuse is shot. You have to compromise when, more than anything, you want things your way. You have to swallow pride when you couldn't eat another thing. And you even have to admit you're w-r-o-n-g.

But mostly, you have to try. Giving up is easy. Making marriage work is hard. You have to try even when you're really tired or really mad or you know, absolutely, for sure, that you're right (and have photographs and sworn testimony to prove it). You have to try the day after you tried.

You have to try for the whole marriage. There's never a day off from trying.

But here's the cool part: It's worth it.

Don't Forget to Have Fun

This is life. Okay, sometimes it's hard. But not always. Sometimes it's fun.

Who are you going to have the good times with? Your husband. He can make you laugh more than anyone else. He knows what and who you like and don't like and why. He can interpret your knee-nudges under the table. He can read your eyebrows like Morse code.

He "gets" you. Who else does?